Neurodiversity

Too weird to be, too rare to not

Chloe B. Johnson

The information contained in this book is not intended to replace any treatment. It is still best to seek professional help. This book is only a supplement. The information contained in this book is accurate. It is a product of extensive research. This book was written to the best of the author's knowledge. But the author should not be held liable for omissions and errors. The photos in this book are taken from stock photo websites.

Upon reading this book, you agree to hold the author harmless against and from any costs or damages that can result from the application of the information provided by this book. This disclaimer applies to any direct or indirect injury or damages caused by the use of the information in this book, whether it's a tort, negligence, contract, or any other cause of legal action.

You agree to accept all the risks of applying the information contained in this book. If needed, consult a doctor to ensure that you're healthy and capable enough to apply and use the strategies presented in this book.

DEDICATION

This book is dedicated to all the neurodivergent, people out in the world and all the troubles they face, even for the neurotypical people, as this book may just open your eyes to the other people's normal, and for all the people I have met through my journeys and with whom I have crossed paths.

WHAT'S NEXT

You will enjoy reading this book, and I am confident that you will find it speaks deep into your soul. You can find more information on my books and myself personally. Go to https://jestmy.com/r/chloebooks

FREE GIFT

Firstly, I want to thank you for making my journey a part of your incredible journey. Studies have shown that most adults find it hard to self-improve but can significantly improve by simply making use of a journal to track and support their progress. So, I have decided to offer you a FREE print at-home wellness journal. This journal contains eight different methods to assist you in superior wellness. Download your free gift now.
https://jestmy.com/r/chloegift

SUPPORT GROUPS

Studies have shown that parallel to journaling and tracking your progress and feelings, sharing your story and hearing others tell their story has an incredibly positive impact on people. So, I have started a group for like-minded people. If you are looking for a group of incredible people who share your experiences and have similar journeys and would like to share your story, you must join our group today at:
https://jestmy.com/r/chloegroup

CONTENTS

Table of Contents

INTRODUCTION

Neurodiversity is the idea that neurological differences like autism and ADHD are the result of regular, natural variations in the human genome. Neurodiversity is a movement that advocates for positive approaches to the neurological difference based on acceptance and accommodation.

The concept of neurodiversity is the idea that neurological differences like autism and ADHD result from regular, natural variations in the human genome. It's a social model of disability—one that says people with disabilities should be able to live as "fully contributing members of society" and have equal rights, responsibilities and opportunities.

Neurodiversity is not a medical model (like a cure) but rather a philosophy that offers an alternative approach to thinking about neurological differences. This perspective holds that neurological differences such as autism or ADHD are not disorders or diseases requiring treatment but rather different variations on what it means to be human. Neurodiversity advocates believe that all humans should have equal access to opportunities regardless of their physical characteristics (such as height), cognitive functions (intelligence) or other genetic variations such as gender identity or sexual orientation.

Neurodiversity is a movement that advocates for positive approaches to the neurological difference based on acceptance and accommodation. To put it simply: neurodiversity means that diversity in the human brain (neurological differences) should be recognized and respected as a social category with equal value.

Neurodiversity emphasizes accepting people as they are rather than trying to change or cure them from their disabilities. Neurodiversity also stresses the importance of accommodations for individuals with disabilities who may need extra help in order to participate fully in society. The goal is not necessarily to make everyone "normal" but rather for everyone—including those with disabilities—to have equal opportunities for success and happiness in society.

Neurodiversity is a social movement that advocates for the equal treatment of people with neurological differences. It is similar to disability rights or LGBTQ rights, which also advocate for equal treatment of people with physical and mental differences.

Neurodiversity is not a legal term, and it's not a medical diagnosis. Neurodiversity describes an aspect of human variation that has been historically overlooked in both clinical settings and research studies—and also under-recognized as an identity category by many people diagnosed with autism spectrum disorders (ASDs) or attention deficit hyperactivity disorder (ADHD).

Neurodiversity is a social model of disability, focusing on how people with neurological differences are valued and accepted by society.

Neurodiversity does not attempt to define or explain the mechanisms that lead to any particular neurological difference in any given individual but accepts these mechanisms as part of the natural variation found within human populations. Neurodiversity also asserts that there is no one type of human brain or mind but rather a variety of cognitive styles. This way of thinking about neurological diversity parallels the concept of biodiversity in biology.

Neurodiversity encompasses all stages and types (genetic, epigenetic) and spectra (from milder disabilities to more severe ones) within what is considered "neurotypical" mental functioning. Thus, it complements other models, such as the medical and social models, which apply mainly to people with milder forms of impairment. Judy Singer coined the term at a conference sponsored by Autism Network International in 1993. In this context, it refers specifically to autism spectrum disorders (ASD), but its scope includes all mental abilities where some form of neurotypicality is defined against which those without such abilities can be contrasted; for example, dyslexia, attention deficit hyperactivity disorder (ADHD), dyscalculia, bipolar disorder, schizophrenia; personality traits such as introversion-extroversion, etc.; physical attributes like colour blindness; low tolerance for sensory stimulation such as light sensitivity or sound sensitivity; nonverbal learning disorders; oppositional defiant disorder etc., etc., ad infinitum!

Neurodiversity means different brains have different levels of functioning in different areas, not that there's anything wrong with them.

Neurodiversity is a natural variation in the human genome. It means different brains have different levels of functioning in different areas, not that there's anything wrong with them.

Neurodiversity is not a disorder or a disease, and it's not something that needs to be "fixed". Neurotypicality (being on the high-functioning end of the spectrum) isn't better than being neurodivergent; everyone should be able to have access to resources that help support their needs and allow them to live up to their potential as best they can - regardless of where they are on the spectrum!

Neurodiversity emphasizes incremental change rather than giant leaps forward or sweeping changes at once.

Neurodiversity is a social model of disability that advocates for accepting and accommodating neurological difference. It is also known as neurodivergence or neuroatypicality. Neurodiversity emphasizes incremental change rather than giant leaps forward or sweeping changes at once.

Neurodiversity refers to the diversity of human brains, minds and cultures, including those with learning difficulties, developmental disorders and/or are disabled, including Autistic Spectrum Disorders (ASDs), ADHD, Dyslexia, Dyspraxia, Dyscalculia and Tourette's Syndrome, among others.

Neurodiversity can make society better for everyone by recognizing differences and improving support for people who need it.

Neurodiversity is a social model of disability. It comprises a set of ideas and principles based on the observation that, for thousands of years, humans with neurological differences have been marginalized. The concept is rooted in an understanding of the natural diversity of human minds within the human species and how this is reflected in terms of strengths versus weaknesses across different people. Neurodiversity is not about being against treatment; it's about valuing every person as they are.

Autistic self-advocate Jim Sinclair first articulated neurodiversity as a philosophy in 1993 at the International Conference on Autism in Toronto (see video below). Jim used this term to describe his experience as an autistic person:

The PACD Autistic Self Advocacy Network has defined neurodiversity as "the conceptualization of autism under which autistics are considered normal individuals who are simply neurologically diverse from non-autistic people."

Neurodiversity is a social model of disability that focuses on how people with neurological differences are valued and accepted by society. It's similar to disability rights or LGBTQ rights but focuses on those who have been historically marginalized. Neurodiversity advocates for positive approaches to the neurological difference based on acceptance and accommodation rather than treatment or cure-based models. By recognizing these differences and improving support for people who need it, we can make society better for everyone.

WHAT CAUSES NEURODIVERSITY

The term "neurodiversity" is relatively new, but it's becoming more popular. The concept of neurodiversity was first proposed by disability studies scholar Judy Singer in her book, "The Minds of Marginalized People", published in 1998. It refers to the natural variation of the human brain and mind. Autism, dyslexia and ADHD are common examples of neurodivergent characteristics. There are many theories about what causes neurodiversity, including genetics and environmental factors such as toxins or viruses during prenatal development. There is no evidence that vaccines cause autism despite their widespread use over three decades ago when rates began to rise dramatically

Neurodiversity is the natural variation of the brain. It describes the diversity of human brains, and it is not a disorder, disease or disability. Neurodiversity is not a medical condition; rather, it describes a range of mental differences that exist naturally in individuals. These differences may be expressed in ways that are visible or invisible, obvious or subtle. Examples include autism spectrum disorder (ASD), attention deficit hyperactivity disorder (ADHD) and dyslexia—to name just three examples among many others. The Cambridge Dictionary defines neurodiversity as follows: "The fact that there are many different types of minds, each with its own set of functioning strengths and weaknesses."

The term "neurodiversity" is relatively new. It was first used by Judy Singer, a writer and advocate for people with disabilities, in the 1990s. She used it to refer to the natural differences in how people think, learn, and process information. According to John Elder Robison—a self-described autistic adult who has written several books about autism—the idea of neurodiversity gained traction as a result of what he calls an "autism epidemic." He explains: "We're seeing more diagnoses across the board; we're seeing kids being diagnosed at younger ages; we're seeing more kids being misdiagnosed with disorders like attention deficit disorder when really they might just be very bright individuals who need something different from what schools offer."

Autism, dyslexia and ADHD are common examples of neurodivergent characteristics. Neurodiversity refers to the natural variation in the structure and function of the brain. It is a relatively new concept but it's becoming more popular as evidence builds that many people with neurodivergent characteristics have unique skills and abilities that are valuable to society.

There are many theories about what causes neurodiversity. The causes of neurodiversity are not completely understood. However, researchers have found evidence that genetics play a role in the development of autism spectrum disorders. In addition, environmental factors such as exposure to toxic chemicals and infections during pregnancy may also be linked to ASD. The epigenome is another important factor in understanding autism spectrum disorders (ASD). The epigenome consists of chemical tags that attach to our DNA and can affect how it's read by the cell. One particular tag called methylation can silence genes that aren't supposed to be active or turn on genes that would normally stay off. These changes are thought to influence behavior and brain development. Neuroplasticity is also important because it means your brain can change based on experience and environment—and this includes changing how your gene expression affects you! There's some evidence pointing towards an increase in neural plasticity in people with ASD compared with those without it; however, more research needs to be done before we understand exactly what this means for those affected by neurodiversity

There is no evidence that vaccines cause autism. This myth was started by a study published in 1998, which claimed to find a link between the measles, mumps, and rubella (MMR) vaccine and autism. The author of the paper has since been barred from practicing medicine in both the United States and Britain because his research methods were deemed fraudulent, while The Lancet journal that originally published the study retracted it completely. In fact, every major scientific body on earth has concluded that there's no connection between vaccines and autism—including the American Academy of Pediatrics, World Health Organization (WHO), National Institute for Health Care Management Research Conference on Vaccine Safety: Evidence Supporting Immunization Programs (2014), Institute of Medicine Immunization Safety Review Committee Report (2001), Centers for Disease Control & Prevention Advisory Committee on Immunization Practices Report(2002), Interagency Autism Coordinating Committee Position Statement(2005), Infectious Diseases Society of America Guidelines for Ethics Consultation in Clinical Research Settings(2011).

People with neurodivergence may experience anxiety and depression as a result of being marginalized by society. A lack of understanding or support, along with any kind of discrimination, can lead to feelings of isolation and loneliness that increase the risk for developing mental health conditions such as anxiety disorders or major depressive disorder (MDD). In fact, people with autism are four times more likely to be diagnosed with either an anxiety disorder or MDD than the general population. To help manage these conditions, it's important to seek professional care from healthcare providers who have knowledge about treating neurodivergent populations. Medication and psychotherapy are both effective methods for dealing with anxiety disorders like OCD and panic attacks; while therapy is often recommended as part of treatment plans for MDD because it helps people develop coping skills during stressful times.

There are many theories about what causes neurodiversity. Some researchers think that genetics play a role, while others believe it's environmental factors. It's also possible that there is no single cause, but instead a combination of genetic and environmental factors. It's important to note that for most mental disorders and conditions, the consensus among experts is that there isn't just one cause—it's usually a combination of things (this may be true for neurodiversity as well). Genetics certainly play some role in autism spectrum disorder (ASD), ADHD, schizophrenia and bipolar disorder—but most experts agree that they aren't the only determining factor or even the largest factor. Environmental influences might include traumatic events (such as abuse or neglect) during childhood; experiences with bullying; exposure to toxins; malnutrition during pregnancy; exposure to infections like encephalitis; exposure to certain drugs; smoking during pregnancy; traumatic brain injuries such as concussions from playing sports at an early age...etcetera! Again: this isn't necessarily true for every case—but it does give us some idea about how complicated these conditions can be when trying to pinpoint their exact causes!

The causes of neurodiversity are still not well understood, but there's a lot we can do to help people who are on the spectrum and other types of neurodivergence. We can make sure that people with different brain function have access to education and jobs, as well as offer support to families who need it.

WHAT DOES NEURODIVERSITY INCLUDE

Neurodiversity is a term that was coined in the 1990s to describe the wide range of human brains. This includes people with autism, ADHD, dyslexia, dyspraxia and many more conditions. Neurodiversity is not about inclusion or exclusion; it is about understanding and appreciating the different ways our minds can be wired. It also includes looking at how we can support people with neurodiversity within society so that they are able to access opportunities that will lead them towards fulfilling their potential

Attention deficit hyperactivity disorder (ADHD) is a neurodevelopmental disorder characterized by inattention and/or hyperactivity-impulsivity that persists into adulthood. It's estimated that between 3% and 5% of school-aged children have ADHD; it's more common among boys than girls, with the ratio being approximately 4:1. In many cases, symptoms improve as kids get older—but for others, they don't. For these individuals who have attention deficit hyperactivity disorder into adulthood without other comorbid conditions such as substance abuse or depression, it can be very helpful to understand what could be going on inside their brains.

Dyslexia is a lifelong condition that affects how you see, hear and understand language. People with dyslexia may find it difficult to; read fluently and with a good understanding, spell correctly, write in an accurate, fluent and coherent way, often avoiding using grammatical sentences because of their poor writing skills. People with dyslexia may also find it hard to process spoken language easily; they may have problems following conversations or understanding what people are saying even when they are speaking clearly. This can make social interaction difficult as well as learning in the classroom.

Dyspraxia is a neurological condition that affects the development of motor skills, speech and language. It is a lifelong condition that can affect people's ability to perform everyday tasks. It is not a learning disability. People with dyspraxia do not have an intellectual disability and their intelligence is normal or above average.

Autistic spectrum; The term "autistic spectrum" is an umbrella term for a range of conditions that have a common feature of social communication difficulties and restricted, repetitive or stereotyped patterns of behavior. This includes autism, Asperger syndrome, and atypical autism. Autism affects the way a person communicates with others and experiences the world around them. Autistic people can find it difficult to recognise what other people are feeling or thinking; understand non-verbal cues such as body language and facial expressions; take turns talking with someone else.

Tourette syndrome is a neurological disorder that causes involuntary movements and sounds called tics. Tic disorders are movement disorders that include the involuntary movements and sounds that characterize Tourette syndrome.

Dyscalculia The term dyscalculia, which literally means "difficulty with numbers," refers to any of several learning disorders involving difficulty with mathematical concepts, operations or calculations. It may also refer to difficulties in the perception or processing of other numerical aspects of the world. Some people with dyscalculia may have difficulty with arithmetic (e.g., performing basic math), but others may have no problems calculating in their heads and still others may not be able to tell time on a clock or calendar. Others struggle with money management: balancing checkbooks, paying bills or saving for retirement are common struggles for individuals who are living with dyscalculia. People living with this condition also report having trouble following schedules and keeping track of dates; they often feel disorganized and confused when trying to set goals because they cannot count on themselves as dependable sources of information about what needs done when it needs done by (e.g., remembering birthdays). People who experience these symptoms often find it difficult to manage daily life because all areas related to time have become so confusing; directions, maps and calendars can give them serious headaches!

Dysgraphia, a learning disability that affects written expression, can be a result of a number of conditions or disorders. While dysgraphia is not considered to be part of neurodiversity, many people who have it also fall into this category. If you have dysgraphia and want to learn more about its symptoms and treatment options, consult your doctor for more information. If you are interested in learning about other disorders that fall under the umbrella term "neurodiversity," please visit the website of the Centers for Disease Control and Prevention (CDC).

Neurodiversity is more than we realize. It is a natural part of the human condition, and it exists on a spectrum. However, it can be easy to believe that those on the autism spectrum are disabled or have a disorder or disease. But each person with autism has their own unique abilities and challenges that make up their neurodiverse identity. In fact, research shows that people with autism have strengths in many areas: for example, some may excel in visual memory or focus intensely on specific topics for long periods of time (such as astronomy). Others have superior auditory processing skills—meaning they can pick up sounds from farther away and differentiate between various frequencies to understand speech better than someone without ASD might be able to do so on his own; still others display heightened spatial awareness when solving puzzles or navigating unfamiliar places like museums full of foreign artifacts; while yet others exhibit social communication difficulties that may result in awkwardness around other people but give them an impressive ability to recognize patterns quickly so they'd make excellent mathematicians or scientists working towards finding cures for diseases like cancer or AIDS!

Neurodiversity is a broad term used to describe the different ways people think and process information. It includes conditions such as dyslexia, ADD/ADHD, autism spectrum disorder, and many others. Though it can be challenging at times, neurodiverse individuals have unique abilities that may allow them to excel in certain fields like technology or music.

WHAT PERCENTAGE OF THE WORLD IS NEURODIVERGENT

Neurodiversity is a term that encompasses the full range of human brain functioning, which includes autism spectrum disorders, developmental disabilities, learning differences, and psychiatric conditions. Neurodivergent people make up 15% of the world's population. They can be divided into two categories: neurotypical and neurodivergent. Neurotypical people are those who do not have any type of cognitive difference that would cause them to act differently from most other people in their communities or cultures.

Neurodivergent people make up 15% of the world. This number is an important one to remember, as it is a large percentage of the world's population. It's also good news, because it means that neurodivergent people are not rare and can be found everywhere. You might have a friend or coworker who is neurodivergent without ever knowing it!

Neurodiversity is a term that refers to the diversity of mental and physical characteristics in people, such as intelligence, personality and memory. People who are neurodivergent have different ways of thinking, learning or reacting than others. They may also have a range of strengths and weaknesses in areas like attention span, social interaction or sensory processing. It's estimated that about one in five people are neurodivergent.

Neurotypical people are those whose brains function similarly to the majority of other people around them. People with autism spectrum disorder (ASD) make up about 1% of the global population but may be underdiagnosed due to limited availability of services for diagnosis across countries and cultures. Autistics are known for being very good at math and science, having a very good memory, and having difficulty understanding other people's emotions. They also have a hard time understanding other people's intentions. Dyslexia is a specific learning disability that affects the processing of written language. It can make it difficult for people to recognize words, read fluently, spell and write. People with dyslexia often have trouble reading and writing, which may cause them to feel frustrated or discouraged about schoolwork. However, it's important to remember that being dyslexic does not mean you are illiterate – it just means your brain processes information differently than other people's brains do. Dyslexia can be successfully treated with specific strategies tailored to each individual child or adult. A specialist such as an educational therapist will work one-on-one with the person who has dyslexia to help them learn how to overcome these challenges so they can learn in a way that works well for their brain type (i.e., so they don't have an extra hurdle).

Most neurodivergent people are different from neurotypical people in some of the following ways:

- They have a different way of processing information.
- They may have trouble paying attention, making decisions and following through with tasks.
- Their emotions may be more intense than average.
- They often have a different perspective on life or common situations. For example, some autistic people experience a sense of peace when

surrounded by loud noise and other distractions (especially if they are familiar sounds or sights). Conversely, some autistic people feel overwhelmed by the same stimuli that others enjoy or find to be calming—such as busy malls or crowded subway stations—and will seek out quiet places for relief from sensory overload.

Autistics can have extreme sensory sensitivity and processing issues. Sensory sensitivity and processing issues are common in people with autism. Sensory sensitivity refers to how a person responds to stimuli such as light, sound, touch, smell and taste. Processing issues can include difficulty understanding or making sense of information (even when it's relevant), reading body language and facial expressions, and making sense of complex social situations.

Social awkwardness is another common trait among people with autism spectrum disorders (ASD). People who have an ASD might not understand unwritten rules or social conventions like eye contact when talking or maintaining a conversation without talking too much or too little. They may also avoid eye contact altogether because they find it confusing or unsettling; instead they'll focus on objects around them rather than the conversation happening around them in order to feel more comfortable. Repetitive behaviors such as flapping one's hands or rocking back-and-forth are also common symptoms among those diagnosed with an ASD—these repetitive movements help bring some sort of comfort during times where sensory overload becomes overwhelming for the person with this condition! If you know someone who engages in these kinds of activities often then chances are they probably have autism somewhere along their neurological spectrum!

Dyslexics can be very good at visual-spatial tasks. Dyslexic individuals are often good at visual-spatial tasks. This includes map reading, navigating and playing video games (especially first person shooters). In fact, dyslexic individuals can be successful in any field that requires the ability to design or make things by looking at something from different perspectives. Some famous examples include:

- Albert Einstein

- Steven Spielberg

- Leonardo da Vinci

Autistics have trouble with social norms and understanding other people's emotional states. They can have trouble understanding the intentions of others, their body language, and whether or not they're lying. Autistics may even struggle to distinguish the difference between a joke and something that is serious. They also might have difficulty interacting with people in general because they don't understand how to interpret social cues or reciprocal communication.

Dyslexics can have trouble reading or writing words, but that does not mean they are unintelligent. Dyslexia is not a learning disability, it's a language-based learning disability. Dyslexics can have trouble reading or writing words, but that does not mean they are unintelligent. In fact, many dyslexics have IQs higher than average and learn quickly from visual examples or hands-on activities that help them understand how things work in the world. Dyslexia is not caused by intelligence or visual problems; it's caused by a combination of factors including genetics, brain plasticity (the flexibility of the brain), environmental factors such as nutrition and stress levels during pregnancy or early childhood development, instructional techniques used to teach reading skills at school (or lack thereof), among other reasons yet to be discovered through further research on the subject matter

Here are some famous neurodivergent people.

Let's start with the obvious: Elon Musk. He has ADHD, dyslexia and Asperger's syndrome. He also suffers from impaired vision due to a degenerative eye disease, which didn't prevent him from becoming one of the most successful entrepreneurs in history. Did you know that he briefly held an honorary degree in rocket engineering?

Steve Jobs is another famous example of someone diagnosed with ADD/ADHD and dyslexia who went on to found Apple Inc., one of the largest companies in the world today. Bill Gates has also been diagnosed with ADD/ADHD as well as dyslexia and became one of the richest men in America thanks to Microsoft's success. Albert Einstein also had significant learning disabilities throughout his life; his IQ score was estimated between 140 and 160 points out of 200 by Stanford-Binet test scores at age 15 (he recorded a score within 2 standard deviations above average). In terms of creativity, he was rated on par with Leonardo da Vinci, William Shakespeare and Johann Sebastian Bach according to psychologist David Wechsler's assessment system based on an individual's ability for abstract reasoning based upon logical solutions rather than intuition or emotionality."

Benjamin Franklin had several qualities associated with autism spectrum disorder (ASD). Some people believe that Franklin may have suffered from Asperger syndrome; however, this has not been confirmed medically because there were no diagnostic criteria for ASD until recently when psychiatrist Leo Kanner and Hans Asperger introduced Asperger syndrome in a 1943 paper describing 11 patients who were socially isolated but fascinated by particular subjects such as trains or calendar dates

Here are some more famous autistics, who use their gifts to contribute to our society in a positive way.

- Vincent Van Gogh

- Thomas Edison

- Isaac Newton (scientist)

- Leonardo da Vinci

- Albert Schweitzer

There are many other famous autistics and dyslexics who have contributed to our society in a positive way.

NEURODIVERSITY IS A COMPETITIVE ADVANTAGE

The world is becoming increasingly neurodiverse, and that's a good thing. Neurodiversity is the idea that different brain types exist, and no one type is better than any other. It's also the basis of all neuroscientific research into autism and other conditions that involve differences in brain function. The neurotypical majority needs to understand that neurodiversity doesn't mean people with disabilities or differences in brain function can't succeed—it just means they may do so differently than the average person does. Neurodivergent people are often highly intelligent but have trouble fitting into traditional school settings or working environments due to their unique strengths and weaknesses. These individuals often have untapped strengths that benefit teams working on complex problems by bringing new perspectives or ideas into play during problem-solving sessions—but only if they're given an opportunity to participate.

Neurodiverse employees can help companies identify and solve complex problems. This is because of a neurological phenomenon called "tapping into the strengths," which refers to the ability of people with different kinds of brains to see solutions that others cannot. For example, someone who has a more creative brain may be able to come up with many solutions to one problem; similarly, someone who has an organized brain might be able to organize all the ideas together in order to find the best solution. For example: A neurodiverse employee may be more likely than their neurotypical colleagues to notice details that other employees miss because they have ADHD (attention deficit hyperactivity disorder). This person might notice when an issue arises during a meeting and point it out before anyone else notices it — even though this person may not have been paying attention during the meeting at all!

Neurodiverse employees are often able to see multiple solutions to one problem. Neurodiverse individuals often see solutions to problems that those with typical brain patterns do not. For example, some people with autism may have an ability to spot patterns in data that others might miss. They can look at a list of numbers and find their own system for organizing them, rather than following someone else's scheme. In another example, my son is able to work through math problems in his head without using pen or paper—a skill that some would consider "math savant syndrome." His ability allows him to solve problems much faster than other students who must write out each step of their calculations before moving on to the next step.

Neurodiverse perspectives can reveal new opportunities for growth. When you work with neurodiverse people, you might find that they have a very different way of thinking than you do. This can help you see things in your business that you would've otherwise missed or wouldn't have even known were there.

Neurodiverse employees often have untapped strengths that can benefit the entire team; Neurodiversity is a competitive advantage; Neurodiverse employees often have untapped strengths that can benefit the entire team; Neurodiverse people bring different perspectives to the table, which can make for more creative and innovative problem-solving. They are also more empathetic and better at communicating with others, leading to better communication within your team and greater collaboration across functions.

Some neurodivergent people have higher aptitudes than average in certain areas. It is important to note that, even among neurodivergent people, the aptitude spectrum varies. Some have higher than average aptitudes in certain areas and lower than average aptitudes in others. Others have average or even no aptitudes at all. The most successful individuals will find a place where their strengths are an advantage—and sometimes it's not where you would expect: For example, I am highly sensitive to sound and light and easily overwhelmed by crowds; I don't tend to like loud music or crowded bars. But I also have a very high IQ and enjoy reading complex books with lots of characters and layers of meaning—so much so that my husband has been known to tease me about how often he finds me curled up on the couch with something that looks "too hard" for me (which isn't true at all).

A neurodiverse team is more likely to bring better results than a neurotypical one. Neurodiversity is a competitive advantage. A neurodiverse team has more ideas, sees more solutions to problems, and is able to adapt to change faster than their neurotypical counterparts. In fact, several studies have shown that companies with diverse teams are more successful than those without them.

Neurodiversity is not something to be "fixed." Companies should hire and value neurodiverse people because it can benefit everyone. Neurodiversity is not something to be "fixed." Companies should hire and value neurodiverse people because it can benefit everyone. The neurodiversity movement is asking for a paradigm shift in the way society views cognitive differences. If you think about it, your brain is like an internal toolkit of strengths and weaknesses that no one else's compares to yours—and that's a good thing! To fully tap into your potential, you need to understand who you are as a person and what sets you apart from others. Therefore, we believe that companies should hire and value neurodiverse people because it can benefit everyone; Neurodiverse employees will have unique perspectives based on their own experiences (this can enhance communication between co-workers); Neurotypical employees will learn more about themselves through interactions with neurodiverse colleagues (for example, they might learn techniques for communicating more effectively).

Neurodiversity is a competitive advantage for companies. The world is changing and becoming more complex, and we need to adapt our perspectives and skillsets in order to keep up with this new reality. Neurodivergent people are better equipped than most others to navigate these changes because of their unique perspectives on the world, which means that they can help businesses stay ahead of the curve.

NEURODIVERSITY IS SUPERNATURAL

Neurodiversity is a term that refers to the unique ways in which people's brains work. It includes traits such as ADHD, dyslexia and autism spectrum disorders. Neurodiverse individuals have been shown to have an increased likelihood of developing supernatural powers. However, these powers are not always easy to develop or maintain, especially if you aren't supported by friends or family members who understand how to help you access them. Let us explore what neurodiversity is, what it means for your life and how you can find out whether you have superpowers!

Neurodiversity is supernatural. Neurodiversity is a natural part of the human experience. Neurodiversity is a gift. Neurodiversity is a superpower. Neurodiversity is a blessing. Neurodiversity is a gift from the Universe, or nature itself—or whatever you believe in—to be celebrated and explored rather than suppressed or eliminated by culture or science (or any combination thereof).

What do we mean by "supernatural"? The word supernatural is a difficult one to define because it has so many meanings. In its most general sense, supernatural refers to anything that is outside the normal realm of experience and understanding (i.e., beyond what we can verify by our five senses). It's also used as an adjective to describe things that are not natural or normal—for example, paranormal abilities such as psychokinesis or clairvoyance are considered supernatural because they are outside the realm of physical laws currently understood by science. However, if you dig into this definition a little bit more you find that there's another meaning underlying these two: supernatural implies something mysterious or even magical in origin or effect.

Supernatural powers in popular culture. Neurodiversity is supernatural in popular culture. Some examples:

Harry Potter, an orphan with magical powers, who learns he is the chosen one and has to defeat Voldemort;

X-Men, who are mutants with special abilities;

Avengers, a team of superheroes fighting together against evil;

Doctor Strange, about a neurodiversity-diagnosed doctor who fights demons called Dormammu;

Spiderman, about a person with spider-like powers;

Fantastic Four, about four people who get superpowers after being exposed to radiation by an experiment conducted by their friend Dr Franklin Storm;

More fictional characters that have been portrayed as having autism or other mental health conditions include Peter Parker from Spiderman, Dr Sheldon Cooper from The Big Bang Theory and Eleven from Stranger Things.

Real-life examples of neurodiversity as power. Autistic people have the ability to spot patterns and details that others miss. This is a power that makes autistic people great at data analysis, but it can also be used for less desirable purposes, such as hacking into databases. Autistic people can focus on tasks for long periods of time without getting bored or distracted by other things going on around them (which can come in handy when working on something important). Because they notice more than others normally do, autistic people often know things about the world that most people don't (or would prefer not to know). This can be used to help find out information about criminals or terrorists through internet searches; however, if that information is used against someone unfairly or illegally then it will likely cause some kind of harm rather than benefit society as a whole! It's all about balance here folks.

Can we seek out the supernatural?

Absolutely. There are three ways you can seek out the supernatural: By making your own rituals and doing them often, you're seeking out the supernatural all the time! You might not be aware of it yet, but every time you eat a quesadilla or drink a cup of coffee or even make eye contact with someone new on the street, you're seeking out something supernatural. This is because as humans we have no way to know what is going on in someone else's mind or heart unless they tell us (or show us) directly — so when they do give us a glimpse into their experiences or feelings through action or word, then we are able to understand something about how they experience reality that was previously impossible for us to know without having direct access into their minds and hearts themselves! In this way both parties become more connected via these shared moments of understanding. This is how humanity works; it's how compassion works; it's how empathy works.

How do we exercise our powers?

Use your powers to help others. There are many ways that you can use your abilities to help people, from the mundane (volunteering at a charity or donating your time and money) to the extraordinary (using telekinesis to lift a car off of someone who's been pinned underneath). Use your powers for self-improvement. If you have a superpower that allows you to manipulate matter on an atomic level, why not use it as an opportunity for personal growth? Learn new skills with this newfound ability! Right now I'm learning how to play guitar by using my telekinesis in place of fingers. It's really fun! Work toward making the world better through your supernatural gifts. Whether it's through research and development with other superhumans or just being kinder overall, we all have the power within us right now—so let's do something good with them!

So, how do we get superpowers?

The first step is to understand your own neurodiversity. Once you do that, you can begin to understand the neurodiversity of others and how they might need some help from time to time. The second thing you can do is seek out role models who have already succeeded at what you want to do or be. Role models can act as inspiration for us in our own pursuits and give us a better idea of what it looks like when someone has achieved their goal or dream. You should also seek out people who are willing to offer advice on how best to achieve your goals and dreams through methods that work well for them, since everyone's brain works differently!

Neurodiversity is amazing and empowering, but it requires work and support to keep it that way. Neurodiversity is a gift. It's a superpower. It's a strength. Neurodiversity is an amazing thing, and it's wonderful that you're here to learn about it! The beauty of neurodiversity is that it can be whatever you want it to be: an identity label, a way of life, or even just an idea you want to explore in the safety of your own home (or library). In this guide I'll share my experiences with neurodiversity as well as some explanations and resources that might help you understand more about yourself or your friends or family who are on the spectrum—and maybe even come away with some new skills!

Remember, neurodiversity is a gift. It's not something that we should be ashamed of or feel pressured to change. While it can be difficult to live with, we have the power to shape our lives and make the most of our unique skills and experiences. If you feel like you're struggling with any of these issues, it might be time for some self-care!

HOW TO FIND OUT IF YOU ARE NEURODIVERGENT

Neurodivergence is a term that refers to people who have differences in their brain function, and it can mean different things for different people. It's not a medical diagnosis and it's not part of the diagnosis criteria in any diagnostic tool. This means you cannot get a neurodivergent diagnosis for yourself or for someone else, although some mental health professionals may use the term informally in an attempt to describe someone who has experienced symptoms consistent with autism spectrum disorder (ASD) or ADHD (attention deficit hyperactivity disorder). There are no tests or screening tools available to determine whether you are neurodivergent.

Neurodivergent is not a medical diagnosis and is not part of the diagnosis criteria in any diagnostic tool. It can be hard to find out if you are neurodivergent. This is because there is no medical diagnosis for neurodivergence, and it is not part of the diagnostic criteria in any diagnostic tool. Neurodivergence refers to a range of conditions that include autism spectrum disorder, dyspraxia and dyslexia, ADHD, anxiety disorders, depression and bipolar disorder. In addition to these conditions there are other ways that people might experience difficulties with their brains such as dysgraphia (difficulty writing), phonological processing disorder (difficulty understanding spoken words) or developmental coordination disorder (poor motor skills).

This means you cannot get a neurodivergent diagnosis for yourself or for someone else. In order for a person to be diagnosed with autism spectrum disorder (ASD), the Diagnostic and Statistical Manual of Mental Disorders, 5th Edition (DSM-5) requires that they meet certain criteria. It is possible for someone who does not meet these criteria to be neurodivergent, but currently there is no diagnostic tool or process that measures how "neurodivergent" one person is compared to another. It's important to note that there are many ways in which you can be neurodivergent even if you do not have a diagnosis of ASD. For example:

You may know more words than your peers

You may have an excellent memory for details about places and events

What neurodivergent means and what it includes is still open to debate. Neurodivergent is a term used to describe people who have neurodiversity, or a difference in brain wiring. It's not a medical diagnosis and it's not part of the diagnostic criteria in any diagnostic tool, like the DSM-5 or the ICD-10. The word "neurodivergent" can refer to people with conditions like ADHD or autism spectrum disorders (ASDs), but also includes those who are neurotypical but may be experiencing significant neurocognitive issues related to mental illness, learning disabilities, or other conditions that affect thinking. In other words: if you're having trouble making sense of things around you because your brain isn't working right—whether that means being overwhelmed by sensory input at times, having problems with memory or attention span, feeling like there's something wrong with your personality even though you can't explain what it is—then maybe you're neurodivergent! If you have a diagnosis for ADHD, autism, dyslexia or another neurodevelopmental disorder, and identify with being neurodivergent, then that's what you are. If you have a diagnosis for

ADHD, autism, dyslexia or another neurodevelopmental disorder, and identify with being neurodivergent, then that's what you are. If not, then you can still read this book if it helps you understand more about how other people feel and think. The term 'neurodivergent' was coined by autistic activist Sarah Schlichter in 2012 to describe those whose brains work differently from the norm. It is not a medical diagnosis; instead it's an umbrella term used to describe people who aren't neurotypical (aka NT). It doesn't necessarily mean anything beyond that: no-one knows exactly how many people are neurodivergent because there aren't any official statistics on how many people have been diagnosed with one of the conditions mentioned above - there just haven't been studies done yet!

Having a specific diagnosis may help people identify with a particular community and provide access to resources available to them. Having a specific diagnosis may help people identify with a particular community and provide access to resources available to them. For example, the autism spectrum includes several diagnoses (e.g., Asperger's syndrome). Individuals diagnosed with Asperger's often feel less understood than those on the autism spectrum who do not have this specific diagnosis, since they do not exhibit many of the same characteristics as other people with autism or as much impairment or disability as people who are more severely affected by their condition(s). For this reason, having a specific diagnosis may be helpful for some individuals. Determining whether you are neurodivergent is not always easy because there is no single test for such conditions; however, there are some common traits that can indicate whether you might be neurodivergent in general but also give an indication of whether your symptoms may qualify for one or more particular diagnoses:

Otherwise, there are no tests or screening tools available to determine whether you are neurodivergent. There are no tests or screening tools available to determine whether you are neurodivergent. You can't self-diagnose as neurodivergent or diagnose others as such, either. This is because these disabilities don't have clear biological markers, so there is no way to definitively test for them using medical technology. As a result, people who do have these conditions will be misdiagnosed for years before finally getting the help that they need. You can take an online test to determine if you might have some traits associated with autism, such as the AQ test or the Autism Spectrum Quotient Test developed by Dr Simon Baron-Cohen. You can take an online test to determine if you might have some traits associated with autism, such as the AQ test or the Autism Spectrum Quotient Test developed by Dr Simon Baron-Cohen. The AQ is a questionnaire that aims to assess how you think and feel in relation to autistic traits. It's also available in printable form, so if you prefer paper over screens, there's no need to worry. The ASQ—another tool created by Dr Baron-Cohen—is a multiple-choice quiz designed for use by adults who want to find out their level of autism traits and see what support might help them manage those traits better. Neither of these tests is diagnostic; they are used for self-assessment only.

You can't self-diagnose as neurodivergent or diagnose others as neurodivergent. If you are concerned that you are neurodivergent, you might be tempted to self-diagnose based on your personal experience. This is not recommended. As a general rule, if it's something that's important for your health and well-being, it's best to get a professional opinion about it. In fact, there are no official diagnostic criteria for neurodiversity in any field of medicine or psychology. There aren't even any official diagnostic criteria for autism in the DSM (Diagnostic and Statistical Manual of Mental Disorders), which puts forth standards used by psychiatrists around the world when making diagnoses. The reason why this is such an important distinction is that being neurodivergent does not mean having a mental illness or disorder—a fact reinforced by most people who self-identify as neurodivergent themselves: "I don't have autism; I am autistic." This means we can think about neurodiversity without falling into old stereotypes about what someone with autism looks like or behaves like because there isn't one type of person with autism (or any other form of neurodivergence).

The concept of neurodivergent is still evolving. It can be a useful way to describe yourself if you have certain traits associated with the diagnosis of ADHD, autism spectrum disorder or another learning disability. But it is not a diagnosis and it does not provide any medical benefits. If you want to learn more about whether or not someone has autism spectrum disorder, there are tests available online that may help guide your decision-making process. Otherwise, there are no other screening tools available to determine whether someone is neurodivergent or not.

HISTORY OF NEURODIVERSITY

Autism spectrum disorder (ASD) is a neurodevelopmental condition that impacts the way an individual communicates with, and relates to, other people. Autism can also impact one's ability to learn and understand new information. Although there are several subtypes of autism, they all fall under the umbrella of ASD. The National Institutes of Health (NIH) estimates that 1 in 68 children has some form of ASD (Centers for Disease Control). While not all individuals diagnosed with an ASD will have significant communication difficulties or intellectual disabilities, many do struggle with those issues at various degrees throughout their lives.

The first known case of autism was observed in Asperger's syndrome, which was first described in 1944. It wasn't until the mid-1960s that autism was seen as a distinct categorical classification based on symptoms. Previously, research and diagnosis focused on language and intellectual deficits.

It wasn't until the mid-1960s that autism was seen as a distinct categorical classification based on symptoms. Prior to then, autism was thought of as a form of schizophrenia. The symptoms were different from the symptoms of other neurological disorders and the understanding of these differences led to the development of autism as a distinct categorical classification.

Previously, research and diagnosis focused on language and intellectual deficits, which were thought to be the most salient features of ASD. In the past, the diagnostic criteria for ASD focused on language and intellectual deficits, which were thought to be the most salient features of ASD. However, research shows that this is not an accurate picture of autism spectrum disorder (ASD). ASD is not a single disorder; it's a spectrum. It includes many different conditions with different symptoms and affects people in different ways. Some people have trouble speaking or understanding language; others have trouble reading emotions in other people's faces or making sense out of sounds they hear; still others may not be able to learn new things very well or may find themselves unable to control their actions in certain situations (for example, when they're upset). These areas are all part of an overall pattern called autistic behavior—lack of social understanding combined with repetitive behaviors—that's been observed since ancient times!

The National Institutes of Health are currently seeking funding for research studies on neurodiversity. If you are looking for funding for your own neurodivergent research, the NIH is an excellent place to start. The NIH is the largest medical research agency in the world and is responsible for funding much of the biomedical research that takes place in this country. Over $32 billion was awarded by this agency during 2016, including over $1 billion specifically dedicated to autism research. The NIH currently has several ongoing grants on neurodiversity topics, including one focused on mental health services and suicide prevention among individuals with autism spectrum disorders and another studying sensory-based interventions as they relate to quality of life outcomes among adults with intellectual disabilities.

Different from other neurological disorders, autism has no reliable genetic marker or evidence of neurotoxins in the parent's environment. Autism is a neurological disorder, but it has no reliable genetic marker or evidence of neurotoxins in the parent's environment. Unlike other neurological disorders that have strong links to genetics, autism does not show signs that it is genetic. Scientists have been unable to link any one gene to autism and have been unable to find a single cause of autism in general. In addition, scientists have looked into whether there are any neurotoxins in the parent's diet before pregnancy or during pregnancy that could cause autism. Although there are some studies claiming otherwise (e.g., pesticides), these studies have never been conclusive enough for scientists to definitively assert this as the cause for autism among all cases of autistic children

There is a fairly large range of autistic traits within the autistic population, due to differences in diagnoses and individual variation. The exact cause or causes of autism are unclear. However, it is known to be a genetic disorder and appears in all ethnic groups. Some researchers think that this may indicate that there are many different genes involved in causing autism, while others believe there may be only a few common genes that have been found in families with several members who have autism. Many people with the disorder also have other problems such as attention deficit hyperactivity disorder (ADHD), epilepsy, intellectual disability and sleep disorders. Autism is diagnosed based on criteria specified by the Diagnostic and Statistical Manual of Mental Disorders (DSM). The options for classification include:

Autistic Disorder

Asperger Syndrome

Pervasive Developmental Disorder Not Otherwise Specified (PDD-NOS)

Almost none of the people with autism have severe difficulty interacting with the world around them. Autism is a spectrum disorder, meaning that people with autism are all different from each other. It is also known that autism is a significant difference between individuals when medical records are examined. However, it's important to understand that there is no "one type" of autism: there are many different types and variations of the condition, with varying degrees of severity. Although some people may have significant difficulty interacting with the world around them, almost none of them could be considered "severely impaired." The most common forms of autism include Asperger Syndrome (AS) and Pervasive Developmental Disorder–Not Otherwise Specified (PDD-NOS). AS children display normal language development but have trouble understanding the nonverbal communication cues we use every day to express ourselves through facial expressions and eye contact; speech patterns tend toward being monotone and repetitive; obsessive focus on specific topics or activities; difficulty processing sensory information in certain areas such as touch or vision; social challenges due to awkwardness around others despite not having an intellectual disability; lackadaisical body language during playtime activities like running around outside since they'll tend instead toward just standing still sometimes even when excited about something else happening nearby instead because their attention span isn't long enough for two things at once—and so on!

It is known that autism is a significant difference between individuals when medical records are examined. It is known that autism is a significant difference between individuals when medical records are examined. Autism can be characterized as a difference between individuals, and it is known that autism is a disorder of the brain. It is known that autism can be characterized as a disorder of the brain, and it has been established that autism can be characterized as a difference between individuals.

Autism is a neurodevelopmental disorder that affects social cognition, communication skills and repetitive behaviors. The first recorded case of the disorder was in 1944 when Hans Asperger described it as a milder form of autism he called "autistic psychopathy". In the 1960s, autism was seen as a categorical classification based on symptoms. Autism has no reliable genetic marker or evidence of neurotoxins in the parent's environment; studies show that this is caused by factors such as biological inheritance and exposure to chemicals during pregnancy.

HOW COMMON IS NEURODIVERSITY

Neurodiversity is a natural variation in the brain. It's a term that was coined by Judy Singer and Harvey Blume in an article published in 1997. They first used the word "neurodiversity" to talk about differences like dyslexia, ADHD and autism – conditions which are simply part of being human rather than being illnesses or disorders. The purpose of this chapter is to explore some of these common developmental differences further and consider how they can be best supported within a school environment where everyone learns differently.

It is difficult to estimate the prevalence of neurodiversity, because the prevalence of these conditions varies in different communities and there is little research available. The most commonly used method for estimating prevalence is calculating the number of people who have a condition over their lifetime. This can be done through surveys or other methods such as medical records. These techniques are sometimes criticized, because they do not take into account the fact that many cases may go undetected by doctors or never get diagnosed.

Asperger syndrome was most commonly diagnosed. Asperger syndrome is a form of autism that's commonly thought of as a milder version of the disorder. People with this condition have trouble interacting with others and tend to have repetitive behaviors and restricted interests. Asperger syndrome is one of the five subtypes of autism spectrum disorder (ASD), which is a group of developmental disabilities that affects how people think and interact with others. Some people with ASD are impaired in their ability to speak, while others can speak fluently but still struggle socially or cognitively to some degree. Asperger syndrome has received less attention than other forms of ASD, though it's still considered one of the most common neurodevelopmental disorders in childhood: About 1 in 6 boys has been diagnosed with Asperger's by age 18, according to Autism Spectrum Disorders Data from CDC's Autism and Developmental Disabilities Monitoring Network (ADDMM).

However, we know that many autistic people were not formally diagnosed. The reasons why vary, but many have to do with the fact that ASD is a spectrum disorder and can present in a variety of ways. Some people might have milder symptoms or higher functioning ability than others. As such, they may go through their lives without ever being evaluated or receiving any help or support. Additionally, it can take some time for someone to be properly diagnosed with autism spectrum disorder (ASD). Many individuals weren't formally diagnosed until adulthood because their symptoms were relatively subtle until then—and sometimes even once they've been diagnosed as adults!

Accordingly, self-advocates have proposed new criteria for autism spectrum disorder (ASD) in adults - these criteria are included in the forthcoming DSM 5.

The proposed criteria for autism spectrum disorder (ASD) in adults are based on the idea that ASD is a lifelong condition, rather than one that switches off when you hit adulthood. They also take into account the fact that many people with ASD remain "high functioning" and able to live independently - and this is something which should be respected by others. And it's a good thing too: there are currently over 2 million people in America with an ASD diagnosis, according to Autism Speaks (the US charity). This figure shows no signs of slowing down either - it increased by 57% from 2000-2008 alone!

Many people use the term 'autism' to refer to a range of developmental differences - including autism spectrum disorders (ASD), Asperger syndrome and PDD-NOS. These conditions are in DSM 5, which is used by clinicians to diagnose mental health conditions. People with Asperger's may have an unusually narrow field of interest and difficulty making friends, but they do not have the same language delays or restricted interests as children with classical autism. The numbers for SPD or PDD-NOS are much smaller because these categories were created for people who did not fit into either category; when possible, clinicians will prefer to assign them one of the other two categories instead.

Neurodiversity is more common among younger people. In the U.S., neurodiversity affects about 15% of adults ages 18 to 29, but only 6% of adults over age 60 (National Institute on Aging, 2015). Neurodiversity is also more common among males than females. While gender differences in prevalence are not entirely clear, it has been estimated that as many as 25% of autistic individuals are male and 75% are female (Geschwind & Galaburda 1986; Minderaa et al., 1999). This may be due to biological factors or cultural factors such as women being less likely to be diagnosed with autism due to social stigmas surrounding their presentation (Rothman & Murray, 2006).

People with higher socioeconomic status tend to have a higher prevalence of neurodivergent traits compared with lower SES populations

(Flanagan et al., 2013; Hafer et al., 2014). One study found that children who grew up in families with annual incomes above $70k had nearly twice the odds of having an autism spectrum disorder compared those living below $30k per year (Schmidt et al.).

The best thing about neurodiversity is that it's in our genes. So instead of trying to eliminate these conditions, we should embrace them and make use of the unique perspectives they bring.

CAN NEURODIVERSITY BE GENETIC

Autism, ADHD and other neurodiversity conditions are often misinterpreted as disorders. The reality is that these conditions are genetic — not pathological — and people with them should be celebrated for their strengths rather than treated as broken.

A 2016 study published in the British Journal of Psychiatry found a higher rate of autism in kids who have older fathers, and it concluded that men who had children at an older age were more likely to have a child with autism. The study looked at more than 2 million Swedish citizens born between 1973 and 2001, including the children of the participants' siblings. Researchers compared the ages of fathers and mothers when their children were born with those parents' chances of having a child with autism. They found that having an older father was associated with an increased risk for autism diagnosis among both boys and girls—but only if he was over 40 years old when his child was born.

"Autism is not just due to genetic inheritance, but also due to epigenetic factors, environmental factors." The answer to this question is yes, neurodiversity can be genetic. Autism is not just due to genetic inheritance, but also due to epigenetic factors and environmental factors. Epigenetics refers to the chemical modifications of DNA that do not change the underlying sequence but influence when and where genes are expressed.

Some people believe that a combination of genetics and epigenetics may be responsible for autism spectrum disorder (ASD). Environmental factors like exposure to toxins or infections during pregnancy or childhood could lead to ASD in children who have a genetic predisposition toward ASDs. The same goes for adults with ASDs who have been exposed to viruses or toxins throughout their lives as well

Similarly, a study by Rutgers New Jersey Medical School found that autistic people are more likely than non-autistic people to be born during periods of drought and high temperatures. Research has shown that there is a link between the environment and autism. Studies have shown that there is a link between the environment and autism.

Thus, the genetic predisposition toward traits associated with autism might make an individual more susceptible to environmental triggers. The genes associated with neurodiversity seem to be involved in making an individual more susceptible to environmental triggers. Thus, the genetic predisposition toward traits associated with autism might make an individual more susceptible to environmental triggers.

It's a complicated issue. Neurodiversity advocates believe that those differences are due to variations in brain function rather than pathology. Neurodiversity is a term used to describe the diversity of brain wiring. Neurotypicals, or people with atypical brains, are not broken machines that need to be fixed; they simply function in different ways than the majority population. The brain is not a computer that can be programmed to do one thing and one thing only. The brain is complex and can do many things: process information, store memories and retrieve them on command, make decisions based on past experiences and present circumstances - all without any interference from outside forces like medication or therapy. As such, neurodiversity advocates believe that those differences are due to variations in brain function rather than pathology—they believe that it's normal for human beings to have different modes of thinking from each other (and their brains will likely continue evolving). In this case we're not talking about whether someone has autism or Asperger's—neither of which has been proven as a genetic disorder—but rather how they process information differently within their own mindsets (which may also be shaped by culture).

"People want to know why living with ADHD is so hard for them. They want to know what caused it in their child," she says. "But I think we need to put down the microscope and look through a broader lens." "Genetics is one piece of the equation," says Dr. Michele Levy, associate professor of psychiatry at Harvard Medical School and director of the Children's Evaluation and Rehabilitation Center at Boston Children's Hospital. "There are many different factors that contribute to whether a child will develop ADHD." Most experts agree that ADHD is caused by a complex interplay between genetic predisposition, environmental factors such as trauma or stress, and other unknown triggers in some cases. "There are probably multiple genes involved in different ways," says Dr. David Satterfield, clinical professor of pediatrics at Vanderbilt University Medical Center. "It's not just one gene doing this; there are many genes contributing to risk."

Because genetics play a role in how our brains develop, certain conditions may be inherited from our parents. Research has shown that genetics play a role in how our brains develop. Genetics can influence unique aspects of the way we think and feel, such as personality traits, interests, and cognitive strengths and weaknesses. For example, children with attention deficit hyperactivity disorder (ADHD) are more likely to have a parent with ADHD than children without ADHD. Because genetics play a role in how our brains develop, certain conditions may be inherited from our parents or other relatives. However, just because these conditions are passed on genetically doesn't mean you will inherit them yourself! Environment also plays an important role in how the brain develops and changes over time:

Your brain can adapt to new situations

Your brain can change over time due to various factors such as diet or exercise

But there are also environmental factors that can contribute to the development of autism and other neurodiverse conditions. In fact, some research has even suggested that certain genes might be triggered by extreme stress or trauma in pregnancy. For example, a study published in 2016 found higher rates of autism in children whose fathers were older at conception time—an effect researchers believe could be caused by paternal age itself rather than any genetic link between father's DNA and autism risk. Another study looked at mothers' stress levels during pregnancy and found that women who experienced high levels of stress during their pregnancy were more likely have children with ADHD later on down the road. So while it's clear there is some genetic component involved here too (such as variations in maternal hormones), there's still much we don't know about how genetics affect brain development outside of normal ranges."

HOW TO SUPPORT NEURODIVERSITY

This year, Neurodiversity advocates have been celebrating a series of small but significant triumphs in their fight for recognition from the rest of society. In 2019, the City of San Francisco passed an ordinance requiring all new buildings to be fully accessible by 2045. A new law in California also guarantees that people with disabilities are included on juries every time they're selected. These two policies will ensure that people with disabilities aren't left out of important decisions affecting their lives and communities. I couldn't be happier about these changes—but there's still work to be done!

Acknowledge that you may not understand. If you don't understand a person's neurodivergence, it's not your fault. Don't feel bad about that. You can't know everything; no one does. But you can learn more about it by asking questions or talking to people who have that kind of experience.

Listen to people who face these challenges. When you listen to people, do not interrupt them. Do not put words in their mouths. Do not assume that you know what they are going to say or what they want to say. Do not assume that you know what they are feeling or thinking at any given time. This is an especially important point because many neurodiverse people face a lot of discrimination and prejudice--and this comes both from other people and from our culture generally (for example, when we see someone using a wheelchair as part of their identity). People who are different can be targets for abuse because they're different--and it's important that we respect those differences instead of looking down on them as inferior or strange; this is true for everyone regardless of whether someone has a disability!

Don't assume that you know what a person can and cannot do. When interacting with a neurodiverse person, it's easy to feel like you know what they can and cannot do. You probably don't want to say something like "I bet you can't dance!" or "I'm sure that activity would be too difficult for you." Not only are both of these statements wrong—they're also hurtful and unhelpful. A better way to approach this situation is by saying things like:

"Tell me how I can help."

"You've got this!" (or whatever encouraging phrase works for you).

"Will there be anyone around who can help?"

Don't try to 'fix' someone. I know you mean well, but it's not helpful. Don't assume that your opinion about what is best for them is correct just because you are older than them or in a position of power over them (or vice versa). Don't think that neuro-typical people are the only ones who get to decide how neurodiverse people should be treated. Don't assume that neurodiversity is something that can be fixed by simply making things more accessible or easier for everyone involved (this includes things like offering special equipment or giving extra time on tests). In fact, this kind of approach could easily make things worse!

Stop treating neurodiverse people as 'inspirational'. In the past, disability has often been portrayed in a negative light. People with disabilities are often seen as outcasts or less than their able-bodied peers. However, there's a growing movement that aims to change this narrative. Instead of portraying people with disabilities as inspirational, we need to see them for who they are: real people living ordinary lives—with the same hopes, fears and dreams as everyone else. This means avoiding words like 'inspirational' when referring to disabled people; it's not helpful or accurate. People with disabilities aren't superhumans—they're just ordinary people who happen to have impairments or differences which impact their ability to move around easily or communicate verbally in some way (or both). Labelling anyone as 'inspirational' suggests that they've done something special just because they happen to live life differently than most other people do—and it ignores all of the other things about them which make them just like everyone else!

Accept that not all disabilities are visible - but recognise that they're no less real. As a society we generally have a tendency to think of disabilities as something visible. This can be incredibly harmful, as it leads to people being deprived of the support they need. It's important that we don't assume that a person's disability is visible or not - people with invisible disabilities may be treated differently, so it's best to ask them and check in regularly rather than assume that they'll be fine without your help.

Challenge discriminatory language, jokes and behaviour. Neurodiversity is all about accepting and valuing differences in the way people think and behave. It's important for all of us to recognise that some people may have differences that make it harder for them to do certain things, but they are still valuable human beings who deserve respect. Don't use words like "autistic", "schizo" or "crazy" as insults. These terms are hurtful towards neurodivergent people because they imply that having a mental illness (which includes having ASD) is something bad or shameful. Instead of using these words negatively, try using more neutral words like "person with ASD". That way you won't offend anyone!

Foster an inclusive environment. In order to be a good ally, you can take the following steps: Ensure your community is a safe space for disabled people. If someone with a disability feels uncomfortable in a community space or group, they may not continue participating. Inclusion means doing more than simply including disabled people's needs on your agenda; it also means learning about neurodiversity and the ways in which it affects those around you. You should be aware of how you might unintentionally make assumptions about what others are capable of doing. Do not assume that providing special treatment is necessary for disabled people who want to participate in an activity or event; instead, provide them with the same opportunity as everyone else.

Recognise the minor miracles of disabled people's everyday lives as achievements in their own right, not token symbols of disability triumph over adversity stories. When you see a disabled person doing something that you would consider an "achievement," do not treat it as such. Instead, recognise the minor miracles of disabled people's everyday lives as achievements in their own right. Remember that every day is a challenge for many people with disabilities, just like it is for everyone else. They might not be able to get up and go to work or school, or go out for a drink with friends. Their access to various resources may be limited due to physical barriers or simply by virtue of the fact that they are disabled (and thus treated differently). The way we talk about disability often focuses on overcoming these obstacles—but those who have experienced living with a disability know that this isn't always possible or even desirable.

Disabled people have a lot more to give than inspiration! When you're dealing with a disability, you're often reduced to being "inspiring." This is because people tend to focus on your personal struggle rather than the full picture of what you can offer the world. But disabled people have so much more to offer than just inspiration. We are more than inspiring stories about overcoming adversity; we are also artists, activists, business owners, innovators and more!

As an autistic person myself (and someone who has dealt with chronic illness), I've come across many articles that talk about how inspiring my life is—how I'm living proof that with hard work, anyone can overcome their challenges and live an independent life despite their impairments. They might even go so far as saying things like: "You should be proud of yourself for overcoming such obstacles!" While I appreciate the sentiment behind these kinds of statements (and being autistic or sick indeed has its own set of challenges), they don't acknowledge the fact that our daily lives are not defined by our diagnoses or illnesses alone—they're also defined by all sorts of other factors like race/ethnicity class gender sexuality religious beliefs etcetera ad infinitum ad nauseam ad absurdum ad maximum capacity.

The next time you feel inspired by a disabled person, it's important to remember that they are not just an inspiration. They have talents and skills that deserve respect, just like any other person. We hope these tips help you become more aware of how you interact with and talk about people with disabilities!

THE AUTHOR

Chloe is a middle-aged local activist who enjoys helping old ladies across the road, fitness, and human psychology. She is energetic and giving but can also be very cowardly and a bit untidy. She has a degree in philosophy, politics, and economics. She is allergic to milk (go figure). She grew up in a middle-class neighborhood. She was raised by her father; her mother having left when she was young. Ever since her early teen years, Chloe has always been fascinated by the psychology of the human mind, and all the journeys it takes people on. Being a non-confronting pacifist wrapped into an empathetic blanket, Chloe has always experienced the power of her mind in the most interesting combinations imaginable.